ACHES

Sneha Pandey

Woven Words Publishers OPC Pvt. Ltd.
Registered Office:
Vill: Raipur, P.O: Raipur Paschimbar,
Dist: Purba Midnapore, Pin: 721401,
West Bengal, India.
www.wovenwordspublishers.in
Email: editor@wovenwordspublishers.in

First published in Paperback by
Woven Words Publishers OPC Pvt. Ltd., 2018

Copyright© Sneha Pandey, 2018

ISBN-13: 978-93-86897-02-2
ISBN-10: 9386897024

Price: $25

Printed and bound in India

INTRODUCTION

Poetry is the rhythm of life. When it is reverberated through words in ink then, we give our own meanings to it. We all wear different glasses, perceive it differently through our singular emotions and our unique experiences. There is but one thing that ties us all, feelings. We feel, though distinctively but we feel.

This book was written as a way to let these feelings come alive through words, woven to become my song and fall on the ears of people, giving life to this symphony. The voice in these poems is not just mine. It is from the stories, I have heard, seen and perceived. Though most of the poems speak of pain somewhere in us, it was created to realise that there is persistence of pain in many people around us. And that, we are not alone. All that we feel, is felt by someone else too. We are tied through poetry of life.

For the people who made me who I am.

LOVE

The only

You are,
The only book,
I will ever read.

You are,
The only emotion,
I will ever feel.

You are,
The only yes,
I will ever say.

You are,
The only rain,
I will ever drench in.

You are,
The only lie,
I will ever love.

You are,
The only demon,
I will ever pray.

You are,
The only air,
I want to breathe.

You are,
The only life,
I want to live.

WE didn't exist

When that whisper calling my name is unheard,
And your soft voice doesn't reverberate through my senses.
When the blush and the adoration in your eyes fade,
Because I don't feel your eyes on me anymore.

When I stop looking in the mirror
Countlessly to check if I look good, for you.
When your presence isn't missed and noticed,
The warmth of your soul near doesn't effectuate my spirits.

When your touch doesn't count as my sanctuary,
And I don't crave for the shiver from your touch.
When my cheek's rose forgets it's shine,
Because you don't declare your love anymore.
Then, I would know, for sure
We never loved and
We never existed!

My confession

Today, I woke up
And I knew,
It was the day,
When I would just tell you,
Without countless preparations,
Without word rehearsals,
Without diving into insanity,
Becoming a titan of a wreck.

I would tell you,
I love you,
I thought.
And I didn't pass by,
I stayed near you,
Where the fragrance of my addiction was found.
Close to you,
And finally,
I mustered up
All my sense,
All my nerves put off work,
Answering just as the humble audience,
Of my confession.

I told you,
That I love you
In words plain,
But emotions intense.
And well, what you did,
Was what made my day,
The best ever to stay.

You came closer,
Smiled on all my magnified being,
My heart crossing its bounds,

Mind stayed over timing.
And then you whispered in my ears,
"Oh! Thank god you do,
I thought, you will never say."

Best Friend

Dream yet bore in her eyes, when she woke up,
Quite pale with what she saw.
Her dream was for real, so implausible,
She could presage a heartbreak, fatal.

His mouth clinching to wear a smile,
The one he bore when he saw her.
So perfect, in ethereal time,
She warned self-breaking her rhyme.

His eyelashes fluttering in disbelief of beauty,
Beauty admired through his eyes.
Just as she couldn't believe that truth,
She lost herself to the youth.

The guy, who could love her all the time,
Someone who knew her even in her silence.
The best guy, she could ever belong to,
Her best friend she could confide in.

He could smile,
And just become a panacea for all her pains.
He would rescue her from her own obscurities,
Making the dream become a reality.

So, she held his hand,
And asked for an eternity.
And he never replied,
Just walked into eternity with her.

Burning me

The breath dripping smoke,
The smoke clung in the fragrance of the touch,
The burns on my skin,
With the wild escapade into the fire.

You melt me into your arms,
You make me spark golden,
In the weariness of time,
And just a touch, seems a crime.

You plough a matchstick to erosion,
You rub a wound into corrosion.
Then when you have created a fire,
You set me over the pyre,
Burning me into my passions,
Wielding my love for you, my obsession.

Time and Love

There are few things,
Which change how fast or slow,
We perceive time.

Love is the sweetest of them all.
When you wait for someone,
The one who is not just some one.
But is the only one,
The one prevailed upon your thoughts.
Time suddenly seems to move slow.

And when you admire their voice
Ringing your ears,
And adore their singing
Through the stares into your eyes.
The time flies like it has wings.

It just tells us,
What we want more.
So why not make this life,
Worthy by loving more,
And feeling the crest of time running,
Like the life is fully lived.

Our forever

This is our last moment together,
The last where we touch the milieu of the other.
The last when we smile and then cry on each other's shoulder,
So, darling let's live this moment,
Like it is eternity,
Like it is our forever.

Dear Dad

I have seen your glasses getting heavier,
I have seen your eyes building mound of darkness around,
I have seen you sacrificing your dreams to fulfil mine,
I have seen your skin losing lustre, your hair gaining grey
shine.
I have seen life seeping through corners,
Wearing and tearing you away.

I have seen you gravitate towards things of my liking,
I have seen you bearing the weight of my desires,
I have seen you working hard not because you like to,
But because it would provide for me.

But still every time, I forget to remember these.
But still every time, I remember the false face,
Of disappointment, to make me work harder.
Of anger, to make me better.

Dear dad, I have seen you lose your youth for me,
Dear dad, I have seen you spending all your life for me.
Just wanted to say,
Thank you,
For so much you do,
And for,
Just for,
Being you.

The deep ocean

The depth of the ocean beneath,
Calling me for surrender.
The curtailing tears behind the lashes
Hid in the existence of the night living.
The defining ache of irrelevance,
Chaffed the smiling face, I masked over.

I was all alone.
I was all by myself.
I was the queen of tragedy,
Living with the king of lost souls.

Then I met you,
I lost my beast,
I lost the melancholy driven heart,
To your sweet ways.

You made me feel,
The living and life.
Not just happy but love and being loved.
Again, When I looked into eyes of the ocean,
It didn't call me.
It smiled over,
And said,
"You have a reason to live now."

Even if it's not me

Serenading through the symphonies of my hums for you,
My words pour of my heart in melancholy.
Not that, I am not happy for your happiness,
Not that, I don't want you at the pinnacle of the azure.
I want it all for you.

All the clear oceans,
All the blue skies,
All the memories of love
And all the happiness cries.

But only if, you had someone to share it with,
No, not those who just smile without their eyes.
No, not those who just clink glasses but drink their lies.
But someone who would have left himself in a beat
Just to see you soar higher.

I just wish you will get that someone soon,
Even if he is not me.

Small Little Things

I wish,
I could tell you,
That smirk that plays,
On your lips,
Makes my day.

I wish,
I could tell you,
When you furrow your eyebrows,
You are all lost,
And you bite your lips unknowingly,
That is cute.
It stops me in moments of life,
And shows me the most beautiful small details.

I wish,
I could hold you,
And tell you,
That your fragrance is
The best perfume,
I have been intoxicating on,
That I am addicted to.
It is the smell,
I crave for the most.

I wish,
I could tell you,
The way you talk to me,
With so much animation,
Sometimes I don't even listen to your words,
Cause I am too lost in the expressions,
And I feel drowning in the sea of love.

I will one day,

Satiate my wishes.
And tell you,
How much you have
Drawn me in to you,
Made me love you,
With those small little things,
You do.

Unmatched Matching

The book in my hand,
Felt livened by the masculine perfume,
To which I associated love,
Cause he used it.
All my senses rose to alertness,
And then I turned to find him
Cross by my side.

I am the girl with glasses,
I am the girl with thick novels,
I am the nerd who is unseen,
Especially by likes of his popularity.

I am intelligent,
I am serious about my future,
But even then, my heart can beat,
But even then, I can fall in the depth of someone's eyes.

He is the guy,
Every girl wants,
Those perfect locks,
Those handsome ways,
But beneath that skin,
Lies a beautiful heart,
That I have seen,
Only I have seen.

I want him to know that,
To see me even with this faceless face,
To at least become friends with me,
To at least smile once because of me,
Nothing more.

You deserve to be loved again

We chose curtains together,
We planned the interior,
We argued about colours,
We sang songs of love together.

We were comforted in our own cocoon of bliss,
We were perturbed by our need of personal spaces.
But we made it work,
At least, for some time.

As close as I came to you,
As close as I saw deep inside you,
You felt an urgent need to run,
You felt an urgent need to push me away.

I know you have been through,
The agony of separation before,
And that is what makes you,
Run clinging to your breath the foul past.

I know it is difficult,
I know you didn't mean things,
With all my heart I have loved you,
So, I know, and I am still waiting.

Waiting for you to give up,
Fighting with yourself,
'Cause baby! you deserve, you really do,
You deserve to be loved again.

For the first time!

The pale of your skin,
Met my rose,
And my skin breathed
For the first time.

Your heart's voice melted,
In that touch,
And my heart wanted to beat for you,
For the first time.

Your eyes saw reflections of love,
In mine.
And my eyes knew they would want to see you,
Forever like it was the first time.

That smile!

The smile that crosses your lips
is the best possible thing.
When my heart knows it's destination,
As if when it reaches there it would just stop.
When my reasons are so transparent,
When my being so true.

That sweet ache of being able to,
Make you smile,
And the sighs of relief
That I could witness,
The most beautiful thing in the world.

I wish everlasting existence for it,
And I wish I can make it possible for ever.
I wish I can be the one,
To make you smile always.

Apocryphal Love?

Tear me apart,
In flesh & bones,
With every last breath of my nonexistence,
You would find my love's substantiation
With every drop of blood fallen,
You would find only your reflection in my transparent.

I recite you like a prose,
Like your heart recites rhythm in you.
I smell you
And become high like an addict.
I only see you,
In reflection of my eyes on the silver glass.

I only listen to you,
Like humming of the air.
I only feel you
Like wind brushing my skin.

If this is not love,
Love's existence is apocryphal.

Suddenly I become beautiful

You look at me,
With all the love,
There can be.

And in a moment,
It turns out to be true,
Not an unjust fallacy.

You ask me my secrets,
Of my beauty of the natural attire,
God sent me in.

I look into your eyes and say,
"It is your eyes which are the God,
When they fall on my skin and my features,
I suddenly become beautiful."

Your touch!

Your touch is my wild,
Your touch is my home.
Your touch is my prayer,
Your touch feels like my own.

Your touch is my haunting,
And it is my exorcism.

Your touch is my addiction,
But still it is my relief.
Your touch is my danger,
And yet it is my safe.

Your touch embraces me,
And makes me feel real.

Your touch makes me insane,
But it is insanely sane.
Your touch is all shades of all colours,
Your touch is the best taste of my skin.

Your touch is my devil,
It is my only divine.

Love at first sight

Heart fluttering,
Eyes in stares,
Warming over an angelic man,
In guise of a mortal.

The question of anonymity,
Defined by the vibe of belonging,
Even without knowing.

The carnival of deep unsettling emotions,
Never felt before.
The unique rhythm of the newly found lubb dubb,
Making my doves fly,
Making my swans swoon.

Wind never touched my skin before,
Like it does now.
As it touched you,
Moments before,
Grazing my senses alive.

The smell,
The impish air breathes of,
Fragrance of magnificence
Inhaling your woody perfume.

And that lovely smile on
Embodiment of perfection.
Those grave eyes,
Making me blush
And intimidated?   Maybe yes.

The subtle husk in your voice,
When you talk to some stranger,

Whom, I don't know.

Yet with the corner of those hazel browns,
Eyeing me wide.
Making me feel your gaze
Over me.

Oh you stranger,
You are
Love at first sight.
You trigger my senses,
Like no one before.
As you trigger this pain,
The sweet ache of love.

You walk to me,
Oxygen stops filling my lungs.
"Hey!" with that husky voice
And I can feel it coming.

The impounding gravity calling me.
I faint in your boughs
My love at first sight.
And this is going to be,
Our story.

Love me

Fly to my yearns mandate,
Summon to me as your senate.
The boughs of strength in my nerves,
To me now your soul vassal serves.
The rain drenches me wet,
The vibe of chaos unset.
Sarcastic winds roughen my wound,
And the satire wet to my pains stand.
The drench of pinning fear, fear of loss,
O! dear, I fear distance between us.
Tear my flesh apart and love my blood,
O! my fear runs in me to rave of our love.

Hug my tears to painless plea,
Dear you! in that vibe, I want to see.
Summon me to the spontaneity of your aggression,
I want to be the only fire in your eyes, your only passion.
Care me not, hold me strong,
Let me wear in my eyes, your melancholy song.
Kiss my pains then, let me lie awake,
O! dear wear me in you for my sake.
Lift me & see me, my attire of shy,
Kiss me like it was our last night, like we are going to die.
Touch my hair, ask me my beauty secrets,
Close to me you be, without regrets.
Caress my hand, ask me if you can?
I, in a blush will say nothing for you to stop.
Speak in my ears, of the fears you have,
Look at me like you saw a nacreous pearl.
Worldly essence to my unsettling thoughts,
To our inner vibes, which gives us togetherness knots.
Sting of pain of my fears,
Wash it over by yours endears.
Beg me, my precious dine,

ACHES | *Sneha Pandey*

I, in attitude & with sleepy eyes say it's not fine,
Am in surrender, you still ask me favours,
Didn't you receive all my summoned endeavours.
I blush with my blood tearing my cheek apart,
Our life song with bliss and pain let's start.
Sing with me my agony,
Coo the rhythm of our memories many.
Touch hard the pain, I face.
I know neither you nor me, in love are enough finesse.
But love lasts the way it rubs,
And hearts to common one lub dub...

You, my only known

Eyes falling over my sorrows,
Can make it vanish.
Being in embraces of those arms,
Can make my heart pound with beats.

A smile curved over those beautiful lips,
Can make the night of my life lit with the moon.
A simple touch with your warmth
Can make my skin breathe free.

A hi! when you are far away,
Fills the void with hope of living.
A look of that charming face,
Bathes me with the joy of loving.

Your voice amongst the cacophony,
Can ring my ears with the pleasure of the only known.
Your love, makes me alive,
Your being, keeps me going,
For now, and forever will.

Am I Beautiful enough!

Am I beautiful enough!
For you to love me,
When I am done with my youth
And the grey comes walking through,
With the scars and lines of time.

Am I beautiful enough,
That you don't see
Other girls with prettier faces,
More than mine,
When I fade with time.

Am I beautiful enough,
That even when I don't look good,
You know,
There is a beautiful heart inside,
Which loves you.

Am I beautiful enough,
For you to forgive
All my mistakes,
And still love me with,
All my devils inside.

Will I be beautiful enough to survive?
In your conscience.
As the girl, you fell in love with,
As the woman, you will always love
Even with the scars and lines of life.

What a girl needs!

A Girl, speaks for her insatiable belief.
Thirst bores her veins & sullen thought evades.
The thirst of the love she demands,
The thirst of her undying belief in him,
The thirst of her truth lost to him,
And to keep her revered...

'HIM', he changes faces
From all she yearns, to stealing her soul, yet making her
thirstier.
It's easy to give away heart, yet difficile to give her soul.
She, waits for her prince, but he gives her, her mortgaged
self in return.
Mortgaged to demands of him, his own vision of perfect
her.

Once a time, he wished the sky, for being her linens,
Once a time, he worshipped, the innocent than the
imperfect,
Those lines of pain took him aback,
For that one indulgence, he would break free the social.

TODAY it's her imagination, he would vilify,
TODAY he belittles her, even her small stupid ways.
Her eyes not gleaming, her face no crimson, yet he sleeps,
He's breathing rough, even though it'll pacify the flame of
emotions,
The rage of love, he once said to bear for her.

Her prince, she epitomized in him, didn't ever feel her
beat?
Her prince, not on a horse, wouldn't take off her
adversities?
The girl everyday inside bears all but his name,

That once old times, they met, they knew and felt the verve.

And someday, her prince, would walk her down,
Over a lane, hand in hand and say all that 'TODAY' u
thought
Was just a dream of yesterday.

Never Loved

When the death of subtle essence of my soul arrives,
When the caress of your fingers fades away,
When I lose my smile over eternity unit of time,
When my eyes look into the mirror to find me not beautiful,
When I sing but my songs are never of love or hatred,
When I cry with tears that never bear you the culprit,
When am alone, yet I don't feel like missing you,
When your whispers in my ears are no more heard calling
my name,
When I can't see your faint shadow in my dreams,
When I don't miss your scent when I am hugged,
When your name is nothing, just a stranger far away,
When promises mean nothing, just conditions with no
heart.

It would be same as
Holding you, yet not feeling that fervour,
Touching you, but the connection broken,
Kissing you, without touch of your lips.

Never being loved,
Never loved.

Loved and Lost

You whisper my name,
Soft yet making my nerves rage,
Raving into intense
Flowing through my veins.
Feeding my cheeks,
Giving me a pink over my pale,
I open my eyes,
And find you nowhere.

You smile and look at me,
The sun basking in your intense love & warmth,
Among the beautifully yellow painted marigolds,
A curve lighting corner of my lips,
And I smile,
But you disappear.

You hold my hand,
My skin burns with affection.
Contemporary of which,
Rises as chills around the burning touch.
I raise my head to see you,
But obviously,
You are not here.

It is just a memory of you,
When you had loved me,
And then you didn't.

But, I smile and shine,
In the light of the loved you.
Cause it is better to have loved and lost
Than never loved at all.

Your Embrace, Burns

Your arms burn on me,
The sensation of togetherness burns,
Setting me on Fire,
Like lying on my own pyre.

My breath is supposed to calm me,
To soothe me,
But it is vain,
Since I am enraptured by,
The vivid crest and falls,
Of your breath on me.

The passion of your skin,
Burning in me,
Fuels my love
For you.

This moment, I hold you,
Is going to burn me
And set me as a smoke,
Into your air.

I am going to give in forever,
In your air,
In your embrace,
I melt forever.

The sky, your abode

I looked above,
In the sky.

And found you looking,
Down on the sad me,
With tears which fell,
As rain upon me.

Your tears touching my skin,
Warmed it enough,
To make me smile,
With your feeling,
You close.

Suddenly you smiled too,
With the sun warming,
On those tears,
Cooling it away.

And love showing as a rainbow,
Glowering your new abode.

Unsought Love

I sought you much,
But didn't find you,
When I stopped seeking and believing,
Love sought me,
As a stranger in you.

Mom!

Woes of living, you face,
Clenches my heart strong.
All the sacrifices you have made,
And all those things that for you, went wrong.
I wish I could delete it all,
If I had a button or just one phone call,
To the supreme, who sits above us all, they say,
I would ask him to remove all thorns from your way.

I would tend to your wounds,
And care for you like you did,
When I am older, When I was small,
And in your arms you held me, your child.

Just your voice,
Would sooth my pains,
And your touch made me feel alive,
Like water in the desert, as it rains.

Ma! you are my heroine,
My first love and my idol.
Ma! You are my saviour,
My only religion & my only god.

I wish, I could take your pains away,
And make sunshine for you, forever stay.
I wish, I could just be able enough,
To fix all your problems, smoothen your life which is
rough.

If nothing is that, I can do,
If nothing is that, I can alter,
I will be what you want me to be,
And curb my insanities, for your tears to halter.

Unfathomable Love

Beyond your sweet words,
Beyond those handsome curls,
Beyond that satiating smile,
Beyond that gratifying stare,
Beyond your satin touch,
Beyond your beautiful voice,

There is a guy,
Who deserves every happiness in the world.
There is a guy,
Who has heart of gold
And a passionate soul.
That is the guy,
Who deserves my unfathomable love.

Feeble wants you

The smoke rises,
As it takes my spirits with it,
Flying without bounds.
The crave for you,
Is rising again,
As it gives me chills over the entire skin.

The reality is that I was with you once,
I felt you once,
And sipped your love in my boughs strong,
Yet falling apart.
You ripped me off,
Making me weak with every bit of me in your servitude.

I thought, I had loved you,
But then why?
Why do I need you?
When I am flying high,
On the rising smoke.

I need you,
The weak emotions inside,
The feeble servant inside needs you,
To make me feel powerful.

It's all you

The sky warming me in its embrace,
The drops of rain soothing my fires,
The wind draping me with love,
Sizzling my passions hot.
The grass reassuring my tired feet of feather soft vibe,
Tired from waking and walking through the rocks of life....

It's all because of you,
Since, you are with me.
It's all you,
All the tranquil!
All the happiness,
All of it.

Should life be?

That flavour gripping my taste buds,
That smell holding definition of beauty in my conscience,
The love in those beautiful eyes playing browns in the
gaze,
The hair redefining smooth lustre,
The skin showing warmth of the heart out,
The hold of your arms around,
The care and the kindness,
That smile which made my world lit,
I will never forget.
You asked me before leaving,
To try and be happy,
For you, for your soul,
To fall in love again.
But you have set definition of love for me.
Even when you are not with me,
Love for me is just you,
It is today and always will be.
I will always love you,
Even when you had to walk out,
Of the pain your body was in.
Even when you wanted me to live for both of us,
But baby, is it even possible?
Cause living for me is you,
Life for me is you,
And now when you are not,
Should life be?

Sweet nothings

I see you from the corner
Of my sight.
You are seeing me too.
Suddenly I become alive,
I remember putting this bright lip colour on,
For you.

You pass me by,
And you smile at me,
My heart stops.
For a while,
And when it resumes,
It honks bizarrely.

Is this love?
Umm! I don't even know you yet,
But when I see you sad,
My insides become dark too.
When I see you smiling,
That day is the best day ever.

I walk with friends,
And you come to me,
And say,
"Can I talk to you?"
And all that remains are just you and me
In this ginormous world,
And in our sweet nothings,
We share our first everything.

True Love

I could see,
Dreams washing away,
In your tears.

I could see,
Hope wearing off,
In the crease of sorrow over your lips.

I could see,
Thoughts of loneliness,
Worn by your mind.

It stirred me,
It urged me,
Even when I had let you go,
When you didn't return my love the same way.

I couldn't stop,
I couldn't see you breaking apart,
Even with all the things you said,
I didn't want you to feel pain.

So, I went by,
Sat besides you,
And you,
Held my hand,
And tipped your head over my shoulders,
And cried.

Love and beyond

There is a line that creases on your cheek,
When you smile.
There is a twitch on your lips,
When you look at me.

There is a tear in the corner of your eyes,
When you see me in pain.
There is a deeply troubled face you wear,
When people hurt me.

There is a happily sated bend towards me,
When you know you have me in your arms.
There is so much love in your ways,
That I don't need words,
But pure desire,
To keep giving you back the same.
This is our story of love and beyond.

I have you

The rambling sounds of my breaking soul,
In a single moment, I have lost everything,
Everything, I stand for, all my work, all my passion,
And then when I turn around with tears bumping,
Making rustling move on my cheeks,
I see a thumb held up,
I see you.

You are not my saviour,
But my companion.
You are not my hope,
But the reality.
I have lost everything,
But with you,
I know,
I will find it all again.

I may be not totally mended,
Who is in this life?
But with you,
I have a chance,
To find everything,
And if not,
I have you as my soul's soul,
Stitched in those broken pieces.
You are my basic necessity to be alive,
Though I have lost everything,
But I still have you.

I love you

You said, "I love you",
It didn't just give me a blush,
But a deep understanding of the feelings behind,
That is the "I love you",
With all the expressions and impressions,
Stamping your voice over my heart,
Recollecting joys and tears
We have been through.

That is the "I love you",
I want to hear.
Not just for today,
But every day we add
Memories to us!

ACHES | *Sneha Pandey*

A chance

Never thought,
That your steps over the stairs of my life,
Would be so steady.
Even when the floor,
I live on,
Gets up higher and higher,
You keep climbing up.

That grit is irreparable,
That zeal is so vicious,
I keep moving higher and higher up,
But I think,
I will start moving up lesser.
Giving you more time,
To catch up.
Giving you what you deserve,
A chance.

Childhood crush

When you had touched my cheek,
You had touched my soul.
You adored me,
But you became a crush never declared.

I promised myself then,
I will love you with every breath,
And I told myself,
I could never love any other girl.

The softness of your smile
The twinkle in your eyes,
I had remembered for long,
When I used to find you in every song.

I had followed you,
I had given you roses,
And you had touched my cheek,
Patted me or kissed on my forehead.

You saw me like a young cute child I think,
After all I was ten years younger and just a child
But you were my first crush,
And even when nothing was to happen,
You changed me,
You taught me how to love.

Drowned yet Afloat

Dwelling beneath in the waters unseen,
I fell into the waters of love,
I knew not, how to swim,
But your embrace,
Saved me
From drowning.
As you loved more,
The water in the ocean increased,
And the chances of me drowning too.
But your love made me drown in you,
Yet keeping me afloat.

Perfect Love

I like the towels in place,
Arranged in parallel lines.
I like the boxes kept,
Matching edges in a line.
I want my man perfect,
With an athletic body and an intelligent mind.
But, I met you
And I found,
Not everything I wanted, was perfect,
Just a perfect heart to love me much.
So, even if you were not perfect in so many levels,
Even when you made my towels unparalleled,
Even when you disarranged my boxes and linens,
You were my perfect man,
With a perfect love.

The beach

Walking with feet tethered,
Fingers clasped,
Watching the sun set,
In our eternity of love.
Glistening sand losing its hold,
As our feet moves through.
Eternity maybe indefinite,
But here in this loosening sand,
I lose myself into your smiling eyes,
Just the thought of our eternity together,
Makes me satiated.
Who knows when the tsunami is going to hit,
But just the thought in your sentience is enough,
Enough to walk me through,
With you till our eternity lasts,
This will be lived in and loved.

My best possible

I look at my dreams,
Turned into reality,
In your face.
In the love,
In the care,
You shower upon me.

I look at my reasons,
To breathe,
To live,
And to smile,
When I look at you.

I find life,
With you.
I find my best,
With you.
Your love makes me,
My best possible.

I and U

You asked, "I?"
I said, "yes! U".
From there began our story of love,
When it rubbed it the way, love rubs.

My, I's
Became all for U's.
My, no's
Became all the yes's,
Only for U.

Now, time took U away from me,
And the, I went away with U.
But what we lived through,
All the years of togetherness,
Your memories,
And our successes and failures,
Which made us trade through,
Make us immortal in our memories.
Make our names inscribed together,
In hearts which crossed our paths.

I will soon come to U.
Since I have also, lived my memories over again.
I will soon become U.

SADNESS

My Melancholy song

I am drowning, decaying, falling apart,
Not because I want to,
Because, it is the only way.

I have an ache in my heart,
Crying, Shouting, bleeding & suffering my poor heart.
It wants to tell you,
How much agony, I am in.
If there was a high on pain,
This is what, it would have been.

You ask me not to give up,
You ask me to be strong,
But that is what my heart is shouting about,
It is not because I am weak,
It is not because I am strong,
It is because, it is the only way for me,
The only option left.

You say you know, how ginormous my pain is,
Then tell me,
Have you scratched yourself intensely?
To numb the melancholy
And feel the more endurable physical form?
Then tell me,
Have you let go of,
Not a lover,
Not a friend,
Not a family,
But your own self?

Of what you stand for?
Of who you are?
Your dreams?

Your convictions?
Your love for you?
And your options?

No! You don't.
Cause if you had,
You would not ask me again,
To try and to hope.

Still, do you understand?
How my head throbs in my skull,
So much so that I want to crack it open for relief.
How my veins feed me noxious truths,
Of my living without me.

No! You still do not.
Cause if you did,
You would not ask me to stay strong.
My heart is still shouting aloud,
It is not because I am weak,
It is not because I am too very strong.
It is because, this is the only way for me,
This is my melancholy song.

I looked for

I looked for love, in the wrong place,
Finding it in the wrong phrase,
Of the song by a wrong face,
In my life's wrong phase.

I looked for humanity, in the wrong time,
Finding it's beats in the vain rhythms,
In the wrong malevolent world posing, being human in
mimes,
Holding truth in all that is humane against, real crimes.

I looked for life, in everything living,
Finding mere bodies striving,
In the labyrinth of complications, losing,
The game of life and in every moment dying.

I looked at me, in the wrong mirror,
In the flowing stream of clear water,
I found myself in a wrong dream called life,
Which I lived, as if it was true, but was all lies.

When my soul looked back!

May be that he's gone and I keep crying all nights, but
tonight I wake up with a zest in me.
It is different, some other dream probably tripping over my
whole personality.
Energy filling me even when I am without love.
The eyes gleaming with light of hope to live, not of the
sour tear.
It seems a different life; I was living somehow,
Or may be dying more every moment,
Tonight seems free and lovely.
Have been amazed by me, so not in me tonight.

Flying, air not caressing my wounds hurting it thus,
The absence of reason in me to hurt myself.
The horrid attire of loneliness, when he had gone,
has left me now.

All I want is to live for self,
For my love to my own self.
I want to live, breathe the air, bask in a day's sun
And bathe with the moonlight.

I want to fly, hurt my wings yet stand again to fall.
At least, it will be a physical pain, not my heart unleashed
to self-obliteration.
I want to taste the flavour of life with variety of colours and
gamut of emotions,
Not just love or pain.

He has gone and I want him no more.
Though till yesterday, I craved for him.
I yearned him back.
But all he could do was give me more of ire
And convinced me through his harsh words,

Not to live.
I wanted to kill myself more every day.

But today, what changed?
Lure life in, to get the craze, the fun of living.
I yearn to dance in rain and touch water with feet running,
Getting to know the free conscience.

Only when it could see everything with life, full of life,
My soul turned back, to see my body left all alone,
Abandoning all, the love for me and once had in me, MY
LIFE.
Only when it thought it can enjoy life
And understood the happiness life brings with it,
My soul was set free off my body!

I became my Unicorn

I believed in love,
With all my heart,
I did.
And then it became my unicorn,
Existence of which, I started doubting,
With breaking of my heart again and again.

I believed in magic,
With all of my conscience,
I did.
And then it became my unicorn too,
'Cause the magic of happiness stayed away from me,
Every turn of my life-road giving me agony.

I believed in myself,
With all of my soul,
I did.
Until, I became my own unicorn,
Living through yet not feeling alive,
My life plummeting into darkness when I was supposed to
thrive.

Fix me, but you can't

You can try mending my heart,
You can try all you want,
The cries of sorrow still hold me,
In every feeling, melancholy, still I see.

Go ahead, try breaking my walls,
But remember my heart will push you out fiercely,
It is not that it doesn't want to be fixed and happy,
But it doesn't believe in happiness anymore, really.

So, fix me all you want,
Try showing me the lights to follow,
But my heart is irreparably damaged,
And I fear when all your efforts go in vain,
It will make you like me, hollow.

Woman

I am the woman,
Living in words of hope and sacrifice,
I am the woman,
Living in all human life with it's noble and vice.

Haunting truths of subjugation in broad daylight,
Comforting tears of loneliness in the night.
I don't need the world and it's grudges against me,
But still I stand without hope for it, as it needs me.

I have been a saviour,
Of people's expectations and inane being.
I have been a murderer,
Of my own convictions and thus my zest damping.

I have been oppressed.
I have been hurt,
Stripped off dignity and pride,
Stripped off my being and me.

I have been disparaged,
I have been modified,
People control my freedom,
People control my reasons.
They turn me into a commodity,
And ask me to act in a particular way.

I am tired of being nice,
I am tired of this world,
Where everyday a woman's dreams die,
And her wings every day cut or furled.

I am tired of the do's and the don'ts
I am tired of the burden

Of acting, wearing, doing, thinking in
A way, considered apt for me.

I am the reason of life,
Even then, I am the bearer of all aches and detestation.
I give, give, give and give more,
Not because I am weak,
I don't need strength from this two-faced world,
They should just know,
The burden of their deed
I am carrying.
Needs more strength to
Let go of one self,
Than they can imagine.

Once again

The darkness fills me up now,
Like light filled me in the embrace of past,
When I knew you.
Now, it's just memories,
Fading into the light of eternity.
Those were times, I knew,
I was happy.
Those were times, I felt,
Alive, with you....

Smiling was easy,
Flawless and reality.
Friendship was life,
A boat to sail through these dark waters.
Love was easy,
True and tangible.

You were the only,
You were my mirror,
Reflecting me,
Transparent through my eyes,
Opaque through my stumbling.
But then life touched us with its thunders,
And we chose different highways.

I am now sailing through those dark waters again,
Thinking how far you have fared,
Tears glistening my memoirs,
From time, unreal.
Wishing you well,
Upon a lonely star.

I don't know where I may go,
I don't know where I will reach,

I just hope,
Someday this darkness will end in light,
And I will find you again,
In future of darkness.

In that light,
Where I will know all.
In that future,
Where you will stay,
There lies my heart,
There lies my yearn
Of savouring life with you,
Once again.
Of living with you,
Once again.
Of actually living,
Once Again.

Just a Reflection

Living in the eyes of people,
Loving the way people expect,
Seeing a reflection of the world in the glass,
I don't know
Who I am anymore.
Just a shadow of me,
Being somebody,
The world wants to see.

No Reason to be!

The heat is burning my tears away,
The heat of anger and frustration.
Tears evaporating with the cold vibe of desolation,
I am empty
Of all conviction and certainty,
All that I bear has,
Only emptiness within.

Mulling over & over again,
From what I could have been,
To all I still can,
To the reason of this sullen chaos within.

Cause I am not what I thought I would be,
Cause I can't become what I wanted to,
Cause I am not what is expected of me,
Cause I don't even have a raving destiny.

So, What's the use of me?
What is it I am living for?
With no apparent direction,
Nor a reason to be!

Good for Nothing

He said that I am good for nothing,
I tried proving him wrong.

But maybe, Just maybe,
His opinions matter so much to me,
That even in my trials,
Even before trying,
Even before the thought of proving,
Even before that determination & confidence.

I know,
I am not good enough,
Not for this,
Not for anything else.

Memories real, Are they?

I close my eyes,
Saunter into my mind.
Pick you out.
Your memories, which are real, which I have carefully kept and decorated
Stashed in the corner.
The corner which is my only thought.

Because when I think of you,
Those promise we made,
Those smiles we shared,
Those kisses which spoke of love's meekness,
Those hugs which lit me like stars,
Twinkling as Goosebumps on my skin.

It aches,
Basking in the sorrow of being left alone in this world,
When you left me and moved to the other,
Leaving me clung to my memory of happiness,
Which you took away with you
And left me with those faint memories.
Which are real, Aren't they?

Cause sometimes, they don't feel like.
A faint, faint memory.
How could I have been so happy?
How did I, ever have you?
And how could you leave me forlorn and lost,
To live with only those memories,
Which seem far away,
Which seem unreal,

But they are real,
At least, this is what I tell myself.

Forgotten

In deep corners of my lonely presence,
I creep along into the darkness,
To be lost,
Never to be found.
To be forgotten,
Ashes turned to ground.

Sometimes,
With hope,
I look behind.
Trying to search for a pair of eyes.
Trying to find some comfort,
Trying to find someone,
Who haven't closed their doors shut.

But as I look far beyond,
I find,
I am long forgotten and into the doom,
Such so that,
Even my shadow from me,
Far behind looms.

Can't Sleep

Closing the pane of my windows to the world,
My eyes,
I try,
But those devil voices inside,
Don't let me.

I visit them,
My monsters and fears.
The 'ME' sitting on my shoulders
Whispering into my ears,
Of how meagre I am!

It reminds me,
Nobody loves me.

It reminds me,
I don't matter.

It reminds me,
Whatever I do,
Nothing will ever be okay.

It reminds me,
Life is dark and sad and alone,
Like the night sky is,
Even if it is full of stars.

It reminds me,
When I wake up,
In the tomorrow day,
It will be the same old torture and torment,
Through and again.

It reminds me,

Of whatever comes may,
Nothing will ever be okay.

So, I just toss and turn,
Trying to change directions,
Trying to count numbers,
Trying to listen to soporific music,
Trying to meditate.

But the 'ME' whispering
Is more powerful than the me,
Which wants to sleep.

Undo me!

Click the button,
Erase my pain,
Erase my nothingness,
Erase the surly past,
Erase my ghastly mistakes,
Erase my troubles,
Erase my smiles,
Erase your passionate love,
Erase your memories,
Erase us!
Erase my soul.

Oh come on,
Go ahead,
Press the shift and delete together,
And erase my being.

I don't belong

I look around,
The clamour of people,
All laughing;
Which I don't get why.
All pointless chattering,
Without meanings and gravity;
Which I don't like.
All vain affections,
Without actuality;
Which I find shallow.

I am gulped by silence,
Cause, I can't talk;
I am not like them.
I am different.
I am still alone;
Cause, I don't belong.

Push you Away

I breathe intensely with difficulty,
I breath in your name,
I breath out in yours,
To pacify what's left of me.
Even then,
I push you away.
Not because
I don't want you.
But because,
I don't yearn for you,
To see me like this,
To see me dying in your arms,
To remember this memory of me,
Losing life & giving up.
Even when I can't,
I want to live
With you.
Die when I have exhausted all
The life experiences there can be,
With you.
But you know,
I have to go.
An urgency from this ache inside.
This is the last moment,
And I don't want you to remember me like this.
So, I push you away.
Actually, it is more of
Pushing myself away.
From your memory,
Your conscience,
Your heart.
To make you suffer less.
I know, I can't be
The rose of your life garden,

So why become
The only thorn on the barren.
So, my love, just bid me goodbye,
Before I bid goodbye to the living.
Push me out of your mind,
And let me push you away.

Insanity Chained

Those pills,
They make me numb.
They want to bind me,
The insane me, deep within.
They want shackles for,
The raving insanity.
They want to numb me,
So that I don't corrupt their society.
But, they numb the sane too,
My sane & insane, interwoven.
I stop thinking.
I start sleeping.
I keep forgetting,
About details.
Those which the insanity found,
In every curve of emotion
Falling out as words & tone,
Of any person.
Understanding life more than normal,
Unmasking people more than normal.
The insanity which was my sane,
The insanity these pills pop away.
Locked in chains of rules,
Those say I am insane.
So, I just let them derail me,
Knock me down,
Tear me to bits.
And make me into someone,
Who is sane,
But not me.

All written in Black

I see my life as a bystander,
All written in black.
I see my love as a third angle,
All written in black.
I see a bird named Luck,
Flying away from the black.
I see myself in the mirror,
All is black.
My shadow & me share oneness,
Cause all is black.
So is my inside,
Rotting about?
It is, it is.
Cause everything is dark,
With dark clouds outlining thunders,
Outside and in.
My life is dark with no light,
Of false hope and convenient faith.
So, it is
All written in Black!

Noise

This noise is killing me,
It is ever- escalating,
Ever- deafening
Of cries & screams,
Of cacophony of voices,
Differing in frequencies,
Whispering soft,
Squeaking loud.

Nobody else listens to it,
Cause it comes from
The chaos within.

Saw you sleeping

I saw you sleeping tonight,
Same as yesterday,
The mascara bled from your eyes,
In streams of lines,
On your cheek.
Hair messed up as some filthy teenager's wardrobe,
Lip colour rubbed more on the outside than on your lips,
I could listen to your murmuring to self,
In soft cries and sobs.

Those fresh red scars on your thighs and hands,
Made me cry invisible tears.
I know it's tough,
But to see you like this
Breaks my soul, the only thing I have.
I know you are still mourning,
Every day and night for my death.

But it's more difficult
For my soul,
To leave you like this,
To move on
From this mortal world
And bid adieu.

Please read me

My eyes try shining,
My lips hold a wayward curve,
My head nods,
I am listening to you.

But what you don't know,
Is I want you to listen to me.
To see all the things, I am hiding,
The pain I am trying hard to put inside.

I am saying it all,
Without words,
I want you to help,
To know,
Without me asking.

I need help.
I am dying inside,
Help me,
Please see me,
Look at my eyes,
Look at the fake smile,
And please notice,
I am dying inside.

Redundancy

Can feel my heartbeat,
Limping through my flesh.
Can feel the missed symphony,
When I think of my existence.
I stray by on roads,
Watching people with causes,
Moving with a determination,
Winding through the blank spaces.
I watch the birds,
Feeding their nestlings.
I watch myself in the mirror,
Craving a life's presence.
I am the smoke which fumes the air,
And steals it's transparent.
I am the life which is fizzling out,
With every limping beat,
Going latent.
I am the dark shadow,
Which screens your future.
I am the shackle,
Which binds your wings.
I am that girl,
Who never makes the foreground.
I am that girl,
Who is too lost to be found.
Even if you try,
You won't be able to pick me.
Even if you cry,
You won't be able to stop me.
'Cause all I am doing is dragging you down,
Into the pit of my nothingness
Into my dormant.
'Cause all I am doing is
Living a life stepping over you,

Living a being, so redundant.

I'm used to it

She looked at her broken leg,
She had tears in her eyes,
While she stared at the wound,
Sitting in the hospital with the
Transparent pane showing the world before.

I asked her, "Does it hurt too much?"
She smiled and said,
"Funny thing. It doesn't."
I wondered and rubbed my fingers over
The tears on her cheeks.

She stared deep into my eyes and said,
"Oh these!
They are just a realisation of
How used to it, I am.
The pain, I mean.
That I don't even feel
A broken bone anymore."
Smiling again she looked through the transparent
Into the world sore.

Disguised Opportunity

Poof!
There it went.
Your chances,
Just because you were not sure,
Just because it was a risk,
You couldn't take,
Just because you didn't trust yourself enough.
The opportunity came in disguise,
And flew away because you couldn't cease it.

Never is anything a simple plate,
It always is served with siders,
But you couldn't reach to it,
Even when it was laid for you.

You didn't lose to luck,
You lost to yourself.

The girl in the window

The hustle of the street subdues,
The honking of the cars vanishes,
The chirping of the birds is silenced,
When the night crawls from my window.

I am still sitting here,
Waiting for you to return.
Wanting for you to miss,
That girl who is waiting for your kiss.

The night entails the darkness,
But my heart is dark too.
Just one question goes through,
Do you know,
In the back of your mind
That a girl is waiting for you?

That extra mile!

I don't know you,
But I am helping you.
I try being a companion,
When your shadows have left you.

I don't know you,
Still I will try uplifting your mood,
So that you don't make a mistake,
In the deep dark seas.

I don't know you,
Not personally.
But I know the situation,
You are in.

I have been through these thunders,
Walked through the glass,
So, I am here for that part of me,
Not you.

I am willing to walk that extra mile,
To save you from becoming me.

Blackhole

I could see my words,
Piercing you,
Breaking you into shards,
Where I could see my reflections,
Over your broken pieces.
I was the reason,
You were broken.

You will get over,
You will move on,
You will not forget,
But you will be happy.
Without me,
Cause all I can give you,
Is a Black hole baby!

The black hole sucking you lifeless,
Tearing your sane,
Making you crazy,
Turning you into the rock,
Washing away,
Corroding,
For my reasons,
For my being.

So, I know these shards will pierce my heart for life,
But you will see me in those boiling tears,
But you will find me in those hitting words,
And try moving on,
And be happier
Then being in the Blackhole.

A mistake

Everything was a compulsion,
The life and the lies,
The clues of mistakes,
At every turn of life.

The happiness was drifting,
Light fading,
Feathers of my wings breaking,
All of this, A mistake.

All of it was,
The fact underlying.
My breath,
My beat,
My revolt,
My surrender,
Everything a mistake,
Like my life.

Wall inside

It is so much pain inside,
I need to vent.
I look around to find people,
People who love me,
But who sometimes become mean
Irrespective of the love and care.
So, I don't say anything,
I keep it in my heart.
Adding other brick to the wall inside.

Nyctophilia

The day shines,
Exposing me,
My freckles in personality,
My inefficacies.
I dread the stares,
I dread that people see me,
For who I am.
And then they will hate me,
Cause I am not capable
Of being loved,
With all my dark tendencies,
And all my dark truths.

I love the night,
There is no light,
Glowing through me,
Making my darkness alive.
I can be myself with my darkness,
With my imperfections,
So, I love the night.

Cause people can't see me then,
They won't judge me then,
Cause all they see in darkness,
Is just a silhouette of me.

Stuck with the melody

I hum to the melody,
That is stuck in my mind,
With you.
Your memory makes it,
More alive,
The melody.

Even when you are not near,
I can feel you with the soothing melancholy,
Of the music which lives with you,
In my mind,
Playing and replaying again.
Making your existence concrete.

Just have to close my eyes,
And listen to us singing.

Addictive Loneliness

I used to be a people person,
I used to love people around,
But one day I was alone,
And in that loneliness, solitude I found.

I tried being with people again,
I tried making newer friends,
But I had tasted the loneliness savoury,
But I was already high on my own world inside.

I became addicted to myself,
So much so that,
In being alone,
I found solace,
In times sad,
Myself, I embrace.

Self-cide

And just when I thought,
Everything will be fine.
The chill instilled in air,
The bolsters placed beneath my feet,
The soft ground asked for a caress,
The swift wind demanded a dive,
So,
I turned into the thin air,
Through the height,
And grew permanently deaf, dumb, blind.

Ultimate escape

The screams escape me,
Shouting through the commotions of depth,
Inside through the insanity,
Wandering through the veins,
Crying for the ultimate escape.

Regrets

The whispers of the brittle bones,
The callous heart of unsung songs.
The only thing I look in the erstwhile,
Is the chances, I didn't take.

The grey of the sulking bristle,
Every pore of the living cell,
Every dead skin with its dead cell,
Looks in the past.

And cries for,
Those incomplete photographs,
Those unsung melodies,
Those ephemeral joys of false happiness,
And regrets of undone yearns.

Terrorism

The world is wrapped with clouds of terror,
The uprising of voices discontented.
With regions and religions,
Coming into issues.
Forgetting that we all are,
Human beings first.

I thought of it,
How it all started.
I read about it,
How it all became,
A fire from a spark,
All some men did,
Was become the catalyst,
Because it was suited for them.

And so began chains,
Of misunderstanding brothers,
Of fighting for things,
Which were only perceived.
And the terror built upon it.

From one brick of all,
To a terrorism wall.

The Fallen Depth

People say,
Experiences teach you,
Better teachers,
Being the bad ones.

People say,
Failures lead to success,
Worst fall,
Leads to the highest climbs.

I know,
It is true.
At least,
I want to believe,
It is.

Cause if I stop believing,
I will stay at the bottomless pit,
Of sorrow,
And one day,
Drown in my own tears.

Even if,
I may climb someday.
Even if,
What all say is true.
I will lose a part of me,
To this dark depth.
I will not be myself,
Again.

'Cause the fall is too much,
'Cause the marsh is too squashy.
Even if I come out of it,

I will take the mud with me.

Dream, Slipping away

Sauntering into the drapes of dreams,
Of ruins of me,
Of past and current times.
I have seen you,
I have held you,
I have lived in you,
My dream.

The only thing,
I ever wanted,
Was to be with you,
In reality.
And with sands of the clock,
Running about.
With the dirt in air,
Panting mere souls.
As I erode,
So do you,
Slip away from me,
My dream.

It is time to wake up,
And see,
That maybe,
I am left with no you,
But just me.

Amnesia

The fingerprints left on the metal ages ago,
The clink of the glasses empty,
The cobwebs settled over the fabric,
Supposed to cover the life from the dust of time.

The incomplete sentences,
The half-read story,
Only the yin of all yang,
The million voices of silence.

Only pitch-black dark,
No spark to see.
The unstitched clothing,
With no element yet formed.
The untold life,
With memories all old and torn.

I remember you,
Just your face,
Just your name maybe,
Just your smile maybe,
But I don't recall our time together,
I don't recall our relationship.

Everything is just incomplete,
Empty and desolate of soul.
I am just breathing,
When yet other memories from my brain,
Are off, seeping.

With but Without you

The wall of the ceiling,
Listening my cries,
Reflects into my conscience,
Twinkling into which are your silver eyes.

The haze of the air,
Walks up to me,
Divulging your beautiful face
Into the strands of whites and black.

Shifting with your smiles,
And moving into me as penetrated by ice.
The clouds whisper through thunders,
Of your voice, soft and calling my name.

Roaring into my memories,
Of your presence in my vigour of life.
The air sometimes,
Screeches through my skin,
And makes the impression of your touch,
Still warm and alive,
Very much,
Unlike you.

The fate lines,
Still read of you by my side.
The heart still flutters by your name,
Honking as I realise the truth.
The breaths gasp through the impossible
Because you are not here.

I don't know,
How to go on
How to move on

ACHES | *Sneha Pandey*

How to live
How to be
Without you.

So, I will keep finding you in every pattern.
In every turn,
Every crest and fall.
So, I will keep living this way,
With you,
But without you.

Mirage

Just a nomad,
I am.
Walking towards you,
My destination.
But as I walk closer,
I realise.
You get further away.
Now I am beginning to feel,
Like walking in a desert.
And you,
Just a mirage.

Drenching in your miseries

Walking into the air,
You just walked through.
Carrying your scent,
Still afresh,
Still raw,
Still dolour.

I just walk through,
And leave behind us,
You and me,
Happy us,
Your fragrance merged with my smiles,
So that even the air becomes happy forever.

Your tears fall,
Fall into my palms,
Carrying your suffering,
Still warm,
But so cold,
Still sad.
I kiss it,
And now it can become happy tears,
Of intense love,
My love for you.
So that from now on,
Your tears well up only when you are happy.

Your eyes close,
Dreaming of the impossible,
Dreaming of your unattainable purposes.
Entailing your discontent.
Still closed,
Still dreaming,
Still sad,

My tears fall upon them,
Cause I can't alter your dreams.
I try,
To become your shadow,
For you to be rooted to the ground.
To become your wings,
For you to fly.
But,
It's too much even for me,
It's too much for anybody.

I see you losing at every nook,
Falling at every step,
Still trying to walk,
When your legs tremble.
But, I am now,
Drenching in your miseries,
Losing to your sad realities.
I have become helpless,
Dying to make it all right,
But I am failing outright.

High

Disappearing tendencies of the sounds,
Fazing out into your voice.
Whispering my name slow,
Even when I am with heavy bass.
I can hear you clear,
I can only listen to you.
Your lips saying my name,
Your voice sounding the same,
As it would,
When you had loved me.
The intoxication makes us imagine things,
We want the most.
So, I imagine you,
And to have you forever,
I remain high!

ACHES | *Sneha Pandey*

THOUGHTS

The Irony of Ironies

The irony of love,
Whether for your kind or somebody else,
Is it can make wars happen.

The irony of happiness,
Is it's only felt,
If you know what is grief.

The irony of success,
Is it is attained only after,
Stepping up from the worst failure.

The irony of life,
With every second passing,
It is walking towards death.

The irony of ironies,
is a loop walking through.
That all these overdone concepts,
Are none free from irony.

Insecurity

You dream the impossible,
And when,
It comes your way,
You get insecure,
And before you have attained and realised it,
You run away!

Fear the man in the mirror

We fear the world, the width and the depth of its
complexity,
We fear the people with whom, our perceptions discern in
perplexity.
We fear the ideas that don't align with our belief systems,
Basically, we fear the unknown, the unravelled,
The road not travelled.

But do we truly know ourselves?
Isn't our own sub conscience disguised and concealed,
Never perceivable completely.
Are we aware of the alien inside?

Aren't we strangers too,
Unknown to our own ways.
Then why fear the world outside,
When what we should be afraid of, is within.

That is who we should fear,
The man in the mirror.

Ever heard of Karma?

Why do you feel miserable for things
That others do to you?
When you are the one who gives them,
That trash first.
What goes around, Comes back around!

Brain or Heart?

Our decisions make us travel distances,
Far from the one,
To whom we belong.
Far from the kid,
We were in our childhood.
Far from the emotions,
We feel.

And still we let our brain,
Overpower our decisions,
Subduing the power of love and forgiveness,
Our heart beseeches on us.

So, are we fools?
To let go of the only thing,
That makes us more of human and less of just brain or
logic.
Our decision to love and forgive.

Assumptions

My truth is not yours to tell,
My being is not yours to define,
My battles are not yours to fight,
My life is not yours to live
And my death is not yours to die.

So in all the assumptions we have made,
Creating us in each other's eyes,
Your assumptions and mine,
Let us add one more,

You are never going to know,
How it feels being me,
I will never know,
What it is, to be you.

Paradise

I walk in the tunnel
Beyond which the light exists.

The light fills me
As I walk towards that end.

I feel empty,
Engulfed by only pure filling my cells.

I look back,
And in a flash, all memories cross.

I feel a tear,
For the ones I left behind.

And in that precious moment, I decide,
That I don't want to go into the light.

I want to rush back,
To comfort the people who have made those memories.

But something has chained me,
Everything is pulling me towards the light.

No! NO! I don't want to go there, I shout.
But as I fade into paradise, my existence diminishes,
Inside out.

No Love for self

You love someone,
So much,
So that,
When they hurt you,
Even then you just forgive.

But mostly,
We hurt ourselves,
We make mistakes,
And keep looking at ourselves,
Through tinted glasses
Of the failures.
We never forgive ourselves
Like we forgive the ones we love.

When we don't love ourselves enough,
Should we really expect to be loved?
We cry in sorrows
And dig deep in questions,
Of why people leave us or
Don't value us enough.

It is just because,
We show to the world,
That we don't deserve love,
So, we don't get any.

Sailing through

Diving through the sea of insane possibilities,
I realised it was not just my will to sail
Through to a particular island,
But also the current which determined
My capability and work to reach
That island
And not land on
Any other.

Stranger than fiction

My dreams talk about humane,
They tell me about love,
They tell me about affection,
They tell me people understand each other,
And care for everyone.

But then I open my eyes to the reality,
This world holds.
The emptiness,
The animalism
And the vandalism,
Of humanity,
Intensification of obscenity
In iced wars and cold hatred.

I can understand no reasons,
No excuses,
No devices
Of sense
Seems in reality.
So, I guess
Truth is really stranger than fiction,
Cause fiction needs to be relatable
And so has more element of reality.

Rust and Stardust

The rust eroding me,
The locks closing in,
The dreams fading out,
I can see life passing by,
I know only few breaths light my fire,
I know only few days add to my memories,
But I smile, for all that I am leaving behind,
I am happy for all the mistakes and regrets and unattained
loves,
Cause those made all the precious moments of
Successes, trials and realised love truly of worth.

And when I pass into a world of souls,
My soul will grain into stardust,
My stardust will become magic,
Magic which lived through the rust of my life.

We complicate ourselves

Why do we do things,
That shouldn't be done in a specific situation,
That we are in.
We make the most crucial decisions,
When we hit the bottom.
We utter the most bashful things,
When we are angry.
We make sinful promises,
When we are happy.
We fall in love with people,
Who we know would hurt us.

And the result,
We complicate our lives more.
And then we look above,
And complain.

Her!

Her smiling lightens their days,
Like sunshine does to a sunflower.
Her staring brightens their souls,
Like calm soothing air running therapeutically.

Her words enlighten their minds,
To become saviour in bad times.
Her care lives beyond the moment,
To become love for eternity.

She is not the woman,
Who needs a man.
She is the woman,
Men need.

Feminism

They say feminism is a weapon,
Which women use against men,
Feminism is not against someone,
It is for women.

It is just an ideology,
Which says,
That yes!
Women are humans too.

They need freedom too,
They want to breath in the fair air,
They want to live life,
Without so many bulwarks.

They go through the pains,
Of the pressures
Of the society,
To be a certain way.

They go through the expectations,
From the close ones,
Just because they were born,
As women.

They don't need you,
To vacate your positions in life,
They just want an understanding,
They just need empathy,
Not your criticism.
Neither your pity.

So, before pointing a finger,
Towards such women.

Know not all are the same,
Stop stereotyping,
And just try understanding,
For once,
Feel what they go through.

SHADOWS

All our life,
We run.
Yearning for something,
We don't have.
Wanting to be somebody,
We are not.
Just chasing shadows,
Till eternity of time,
We run.

UNCERTAINTY

And just when you have done something,
You know, can change your life.
The thing, which has the ability to,
Make you soar or fall trying.

You are not sure anymore....

Trance

All that we dream of,
All that we smile for,
All that we yearn,
All that we live for,
All our reasons and our being,
Is mere trance of the decaying body.

Success and Pride!

The high tide of time is a test,
You are put through.
If you stay with your roots,
And you keep your armour of humility on,
You have passed.

But If you succumb to the baloney of success,
The pride it brings with it,
You are vain and shallow,
You don't deserve to win, Not at all!

Freedom

Escaping from the facade of society,
My soul wants to get free.

Fly without ties,
Run without leashes,
Unravelling the true sense of freedom,
Thwarting the bondages of rules and regulations,
Of how to act and how to be.

I want to be myself,
The innate energy filling through,
Space and times in which I exist.

Questioning reasons of life,
Defining abstract tendencies.
Not just feeling self escalation,
Through what people think of me.

Not just by abiding by the formulae,
Man has come up with,
On how to live.

That in the real sense would be freedom!

Our Closets

A window evincing the reality you hold,
We all have our closets inside.

Where we hide from the existence we are carved with,
Where the truth of our living and way of it actually sprawls.
Where the secret is so dark, even our conscience has no
light.
Where we are demons to our own angels,
Where we manipulate our own vulnerabilities.

When those weaknesses show themselves, that closet is
gaped,
And then we find our demon escaped.
Revealing us in the selfish skin we wear,
From the closet, to the world we fear.

In the face of the villain we hold
And a heart where every emotion is banality,
All altruism cold.

Why ask me to be real?

You ask me
To be myself.
And then,
When I am myself,
You scan me,
You pick out my flaws,
You disintegrate me like a case study,
You peek into my 'Me' space,
You criticise my moves,
Categorise me like books on your shelf.
Give me names,
You make me feel good for nothing.
Then why the hell,
Do you ask me to be myself?
Why do you ask me to be real?

To be Happy, we lie

Past is just a story,
We say to ourselves.
Whether the glass,
Was half empty or half filled.
It is just what we
Say to our conscience.
The truth is what we make true,
By telling it to ourselves again and again.
Whatever we enforce,
Stays as truth in our memory.
An unhappy man has
Half empty glasses,
A truth today that is
Full of truths of yesterday,
And a past for that matter.
A happy man has just todays,
A half filled glass,
A promise of happy tomorrow,
And today's truth filled with
Lies of yesterday.

I am a sceptic or am I not.

I am a sceptic,
With the fad & the false,
Encircling your being,
With the fool & the forlorn,
Preaching your name.

With the signs of the signs,
Of the world burning
With its created fire,
With the agony & suffering,
Of people, you made.

So, if not to prove me wrong,
Then to just prove other's belief right,
Tend, Mend
The scars,
Of every other child,
Of every other woman,
Of every other man,
Wounded by others like them,
Like your own body
Hurting itself.

And that would be enough,
To make me a believer,
Not that you care much,
But do for the people who believe,
Do it for the part in me,
Which wants to believe,
Even with all the facade and affliction.

Three!

The black,
The fire,
The ash.

The sun,
The rain,
The bow across the horizon.

The smoke,
The fog,
The smog.

The being,
The decay,
The extinct.

The black,
The white,
The grey.

Me,
You,
Unreal.

The angel,
The demon,
The man.

The man,
The earth,
The misuse.

The choke,
The endure,

The life.

Fake Eyes!

Wondering at the ages
Of the lines which form her
Smile.
Wondering about those smiles
Which never are found in her eyes.
Wondering about
Where she lost herself.
Wondering if it all is fake or it is all real.

I am talking about her,
The girl I have seen growing,
Since I have understood the meaning of life.
I am talking about her fake smile,
Which never reflects in her eyes.
I am talking about the girl
I know inside out,
Yet, I feel she surprises me
With newer dimensions every time.

So, I asked this girl,
"Why are your smiles fake?"
She answered with a real smile,
"Maybe it is just the eyes which are!"
And I looked at her eyes again,
In the mirror.

I found that she was just a carve
Of somebody I always
Taught her to be,
Yes! I am talking about me.

Renegade

I am crazy,
Cause I never walk on the paths travelled.
I am the outcast,
Cause my opinions and expressions matter to me.
I am a rebel,
Cause I see different notions than normal.
I am different,
Cause I see opportunity in failures.
I am a reformer,
Cause I choose to make new ideas work.
I am empathetic,
Cause I put myself in your shoes.
I am the change maker,
Cause I take risks in proportions.

I may not be you,
But I am not bad,
Cause everybody is renegade
In some capacity.
It is just us who accept ourselves,
The way we are,
And become
Unique from stale.

I am a Mystery

What?
You say,
I am complicated.
You say,
You can't understand me.
You say,
I am a mystery.

Well baby!
Enjoy it.
Cause trust me,
You don't want to know,
What's going inside my maze.
Cause trust me,
You don't want to understand my seed.
Cause be sure,
You don't want to unravel the mystery.

Knowing Self

The drip of sweat running through my skin,
In my senate it gives diversity.
To thoughts and feelings,
To the realization in soul numbing.

The music so loud,
Making my insides turn out,
Crumbling paradoxes,
Wavering themes,
Themes of my existence,
In different parallels.
The complexity becomes
So cognizant,
Simplicity in reality.

I know what is going inside,
The troubled falsities and real issues apart,
I know myself more than ever.
That's what the high on rage gives me,
Understanding of my own complex.
Knowing my own self.

Paint it White!

My mistakes turned the canvas black,
I had no point of making more,
No point of return.
What could I do?
I had to make more inked black on the canvas of my life.

So I bought a white poster colour,
And rubbed it in.
Cause if I don't
I wont commit more mistakes,
I won't grow,
I won't be alive,
I won't live like me.

I painted my blackened canvas white!
And now it was pale
With a snowy board for more mistakes and life.
Spotless, clean.... Bright.

Not Permanent

Happiness is not permanent,
So we learn to tread through the sorrows.
Life isn't permanent either,
But we don't really
Learn to endure it.
We just whine and complain,
But for all life is that way.
All we need to do is,
Accept it and live through.

Childhood

There was a time,
When I needed no music to groove.
When I could laugh without inhibitions.
When I was happy without an apparent reason.
When just a smile of my crush made my day.

A time when I was looking forward for more challenges.
When everything was going to be all right in minutes.
When I loved everybody.
When I was carefree and
I had no intentions of judging people,
And I was living life,
As it is supposed to live.

Voice

I may just say,
What has already been told.
But my voice will be different,
Newer words construed,
Together in a different weave.

'Cause my voice is one,
And only.
It may not be what you want to listen,
It may not be what you thought you would listen,
But it will be,
Unique.
And a lone
In the world of knit voices
Hanging in threads
Of ideas.

Cause it will be my thought,
In my own words,
In my very own,
Voice.

Frequency

We believe in different things.
We lead different lives.
We make different choices,
We word different voices.

The frequency of your belief,
And mine,
May not be the same.
But our frequencies,
Walked in the same wave
For a while.

And that is how,
We made a life,
Where our frequencies,
Worked for each other.

Washed Away

The washed off pages,
Torn on the sides.
The greying mane,
Wore sadness in the braid.
Diminishing vision,
From the melting eyes,
Forgotten smile,
On lips a drought.

If it was easy,
He could have stayed young.
If it was easy,
He could have been happy.
If it was easy,
It could never have been life.

Rivalry of tragedy

We all have tragedies,
We all have our own marsh of mess,
Surrounded by the vixen disappointment,
Or the falling apart of true reason.

Emotional, Social, Physical, Financial.
The varied needs of milieu,
But, I don't really understand,
How one is bigger than the other.

We say, we understand,
But do we?
We say, we have deeper marshes,
But do we extrapolate where we stand on the scale?

If ours is worse,
There are many others,
Figuring ways out of,
More than worse.

So who gives us right,
To define the intensity,
Of what our fellow residents of the mother,
Go through.

We don't know them.
Maybe,
They are going through much more,
Than what their existences can bear.

It is not about intensities,
Or competition of tragedies,
Which I often tend to see around,
In every I.

It is about acceptance,
And empathy
That whatever we face,
We need to understand.
If not, feel the paths,
Of others,
Beyond faces of rivalry.

False Monks

There are wolves around us,
Wearing skins of sheep.
There are animals raving,
Underneath the masks of humanity.
There are claws clasped in attire of normal,
There are fangs which smile as teeth.

They are somebody else.
They may have grown to be civilised.
But they are just false monks,
Preaching false songs.
Living fake lives,
Acting to bear unreal unbearable rife.
Beware!
They may be around you.
Beware!
They may be,
Actually in you.

Streaming Life

Sometimes I feel like my life is streaming.
Some teenager movie watching,
Or some god dreaming,
In some other dimension still buffering.

I am just a character,
Or a puppet
Of plans pre-decided,
Of stories where I am chided.

Am I really independent,
Of thought and actions,
Or just I am losing my dimensions of thinking,
To insane proclivities, in the continuum factions.

I don't know yet,
But for thinking sake,
Just for juggling in my processes,
To think of it,
It would be fun,
If somebody did tell me
In this life,
How to run!

The Imperfect Diamond

He cut it into angles,
Of defining sparkles.
He polished the sides,
To perfect the elegance.
Yet, for him,
It was not perfect,
So, he kept going,
Kept on working.

The stone had a personality,
Which was not like any other,
The stone had an individuality,
Which bred away from perfection.
The very perfect that stone could become,
Was in its imperfection.

So, the maker realised,
That how much so ever,
He wanted the stone to outshine,
But one simply can't alter a character.
One simply can't alter the soul.
So, he let the stone be,
And the stone became,
One of the most precious jewels,
He had made.

What went wrong?

There was a time,
When I stared at the stars,
And promised myself,
One day, I will get out of the dark.

There was a time,
Not long ago,
I knew my plans,
Would come into my future being true.

I made castles in the air,
Of imagination of the coming,
I lived with hope between my breath,
I lived with a promise not real.

Today, I look back,
And ask myself,
Where did I go wrong?
What happened?
What caused the withering storm?
And the wiser me,
Holds no promise of future,
Holds no faith in the unreal,
Embraces darkness as a crony
And says to me,
"It is just life,
It screws you, that's all!"

Randomness

There is but,
The deeper meaning of randomness.
It prevails,
Over every distant second we have played.

Our existences forwarding into myths,
Futures pledging into secrets of fate.
Some reason to choose some pathways,
Some excuses for our egos to sate.

But look closer,
Think deeper,
And you won't find a pattern,
Neither will there be a cause.

Our existences are just random,
Between spaces and darkness and light.
Our causes and bulwarks just beauty of chaos,
Laying in the tantrums of what might.

We may become who we wanted,
We may achieve what we dream.
But ultimately it is all randomness,
And getting something we yearn,
Just inane probability.

Shakti

Every voice,
Every thought,
Every conscience,
Every breath,
Is hers.
The life in every cell of living,
The manifestation of existence forming.
The gentle and the loving,
The fierce but forgiving.
Is all her.
You see her everyday.
The fire in her eyes,
The determined will to break free,
The swirling wind of ambition in her wings,
The burning passion to soar high.
But,
She is crushed,
By the social rules of,
Her inferiority.
By the very own essence of the world,
She filled with passion.
By the very own life,
She created.
Even then,
She picks herself up,
Makes your house, home again.
She nourishes you,
With the zeal of life.
She works tirelessly,
For her dreams,
And still makes your life comfortable.
She gives you,
The shelter of motherhood.
She is strong,

She doesn't give up,
Not on her dreams,
Never on you.
She is your mother,
Being your saviour, soothing your pain.
She is your friend,
Listening to you even when you don't say.
She is your sister,
Playfully warming up your heart.
She is your wife,
With just a smile, wearing out the tire of your day.
She is your daughter,
Who is there no matter what.
She completes you,
She completes Shiva,
She is Shakti.
The verve of creation,
The one who made life possible,
She is the woman.

64502201R00099

Made in the USA
Middletown, DE
14 February 2018